Sacred times

Sacred times

OUR FIRST CELEBRATIONS OF

RECONCILIATION

AND

EUCHARIST

LoyolaPress.

3441 N. Ashland Avenue
Chicago, Illinois 60657
(800) 621-1008
LoyolaEducationGroup.org

This book was written by Jane E. Regan and Mimi McReavy Bitzan as a component of *Gathering Together: First Celebrations of Reconciliation and Eucharist, A Family Preparation Program.*

Cover design by Eva Vincze and Karen Christoffersen
Interior design by Eva Vincze

ISBN: 0-8294-1939-X

Printed in the United States of America.
03 04 05 06 07 08 09 10 Bang 10 9 8 7 6 5 4 3 2 1

contents

✳

note to parents…

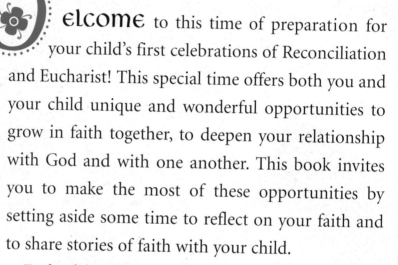

Welcome to this time of preparation for your child's first celebrations of Reconciliation and Eucharist! This special time offers both you and your child unique and wonderful opportunities to grow in faith together, to deepen your relationship with God and with one another. This book invites you to make the most of these opportunities by setting aside some time to reflect on your faith and to share stories of faith with your child.

Each of the themes in this book is designed to help you make connections between your faith, your life, and the life of your family. Each theme reflects the dialogue that is at the heart of our relationship with God. It is a dialogue initiated by God—an invitation to which we respond.

God's invitation

Each theme begins with an invitation to reflect on some aspect of the sacraments—forgiveness, gratitude, belonging—and the ways in which this is experienced in your life and the life of your family.

An exploration of the teaching of the Church helps you look more closely at your own understanding of the sacraments, particularly Penance and Eucharist.

The reflection on a reading from Scripture develops the ways God's Word is an invitation to us, an invitation given in love.

Our response

In light of the teachings of the Church and the invitation of God through Scripture, the closing of each theme gives you an opportunity to name ways you and your family can respond.

More than simply a resource to use for this time of preparation, this book also serves as a place to collect memories. Space is provided for you to express the care and love that you feel for your child and to write about meaningful insights and experiences you want to share.

May this time of preparation
be a special time, a sacred time,
for your child and for you.

Theme 1
sacraments: celebrations of god's love

From the time the family gets up in the morning until the final light is turned off at the end of the day, parents express their love for their children in many ways. And children—from the clear "I love you!" to the less explicit acts of kindness—use words, gestures, and actions to convey their love as well.

Sit quietly for a few moments and reflect on the past couple of days. Name some of the ways you conveyed your love to your child who is preparing for first celebrations of Reconciliation and of Eucharist.

Now remember

the ways in which

this child expresses love to you.

Name your favorites.

5

Seven sacraments—one reality

While each of the seven sacraments has its own focus and place in the life of the believer and of the community of faith, they all point to the same reality: Sacraments are celebrations of what God has done and continues to do in the life of the Christian community.

Each time we celebrate a sacrament we celebrate God's presence and love. The sacraments give us an image of who God is and what God hopes for us.

The sacraments are first and foremost celebrations of the Church. In uniting us with Christ, they strengthen our relationships with each other in the local community. It is within the context of the community celebration of the sacraments that we come to know ourselves as a people united in God and called to be witnesses of his love to the world.

Our everyday experiences of belonging, loving, forgiving, and sharing meals help shape our understanding of the sacraments. And celebrating the sacraments gives us a renewed sense of how we are to live our lives. When we celebrate Eucharist, for example, we are reminded of our unity with God and with others in the death and Resurrection of Jesus. We are then sent forth from the celebration of Eucharist challenged to live with a greater awareness of that unity. When we celebrate reconciliation, we experience God's forgiveness and are reminded that God has empowered us to live lives that reflect that same forgiveness—to be people, parents, spouses, friends who forgive as God forgives.

The sacraments tell the world who we are and who we hope to be—a community that lives in God's love and reflects that love to others.

Reflection on the acts of the apostles

They devoted themselves to the teaching of the apostles and to the communal life, to the breaking of the bread and to the prayers. . . . All who believed were together and had all things in common; they would sell their property and possessions and divide them among all according to each one's need. Every day they devoted themselves to meeting together in the temple area and to breaking bread in their homes.

ACTS 2:42–46A

In the Acts of the Apostles, Luke presents us with a picture of the first Christian community.

Within your parish, your community of faith, you and your family experience and give expression to God's presence just as the first Christian community did. You and your family are part of a wider community, a parish community, whose members support you with prayer and with positive examples of living lives that reflect God's presence and love.

❋

The grace of the sacraments
is similar to the grace of parenting—
when we need new and renewed strength,
God is present.

this time of preparation provides an important opportunity for you to reflect on your connection with your parish. It gives you the chance to strengthen your family's ties with the parish by making a commitment to

* Attend weekend liturgy at your parish with your family
* Get to get to know those who worship with you
* Sign up to serve in a parish ministry
* Plan to attend parish social events as a family

What one commitment will you make to strengthen your family's ties to your parish this year?

Making this a sacred time

Not only is this a good time to reflect on your connection with the parish, this period of preparation also gives your family an opportunity to make this a special time, a sacred time for your family. Talk with your son or daughter about some ways in which you hope that this can be a special time for your family. Expressing these hopes as specific actions you'll take as a family is a good start. Consider the following possibilities:

* Make one night a week a special family dinner night.
* Participate fully at Mass each weekend.
* Pray together before your meals.
* Read stories about Jesus together.
* Decide on a way that your family can be of service to others.
* Take time to pray with your child before bedtime.
* Invite your child's godparents to take part in this time of preparation.

To make this a sacred time, our family will

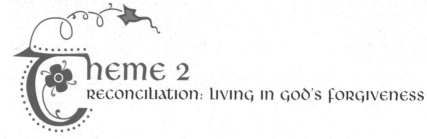

Theme 2
Reconciliation: Living in God's Forgiveness

Preparing your child to celebrate the Sacrament of Penance and Reconciliation for the first time gives you the opportunity to reflect on your understanding and experience of forgiveness and reconciliation in your own life. In countless ways, you pass along your perceptions and understandings to your children.

Reflect on each of the following quotations:

"Forgiveness is not an occasional act: it is a permanent attitude."
MARTIN LUTHER KING, JR.

"We do not really know how to forgive until we know what it is to be forgiven. Therefore we should be glad that we can be forgiven by others. It is our forgiveness of one another that makes the love of Jesus manifest in our lives, for in forgiving one another we act toward one another as he has acted towards us."
THOMAS MERTON

"Because God is a forgiving God, we must become forgiving people if we are to be his children."
GEORGE MARTIN

"To forgive is divine. The first step for us is to acknowledge our own inability to forgive and to beg God to take over and forgive within us."
GERARD W. HUGHES

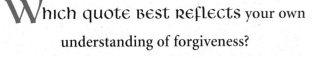

Which quote best reflects your own understanding of forgiveness?

What would you like your child to learn from you about forgiveness and reconciliation?

The Sacrament of Penance celebrates God's love and ever-present forgiveness. It calls us to live our lives as Jesus did—with compassion and understanding. We are called to be merciful—to forgive one another as God forgives us. God's love and forgiveness are limitless.

Practicing Forgiveness

In his teaching and in the way he lived his life, Jesus shows us that forgiveness is an ongoing process. Yet, experiencing forgiveness and reconciliation is often difficult for us. When we ask for forgiveness, we openly admit our weakness to others. When we extend forgiveness, we have to let go of anger, frustration, old grudges, and deep hurts. This requires a great amount of energy, trust, courage, and strength.

As Christians, our faith can help us find the strength we need to be people of forgiveness. Consider three practices that are central elements of our Catholic tradition:

✳ **Prayer:** Spending time in personal prayer is a great help in overcoming the pain of past hurts and anger. In prayer, we quiet our troubled spirits and open ourselves to the peace and grace of God's Spirit.

✳ **Eucharist:** Celebrating the Eucharist every week helps us be open to the grace we need to be people of forgiveness and reconciliation. At the beginning of our Eucharistic celebration, we take time to examine our lives and to ask for God's mercy. During the Eucharist, we extend Christ's peace to one another, and we are sent forth to serve and to bring Christ's love to the world.

✳ **Reconciliation:** Celebrating the Sacrament of Penance and Reconciliation makes us more aware of God's ever-present love and forgiveness, and helps us live with renewed commitment, deeper faith, and greater insight.

Think About It: As you reflect on important experiences of forgiveness in your life, what has given you the strength to forgive or to ask for forgiveness?

Reflection on the Gospel of Mark

When Jesus returned to Capernaum after some days, it became known that he was at home. Many gathered together so that there was no longer room for them, not even around the door, and he preached the word to them. They came bringing to him a paralytic carried by four men. Unable to get near Jesus because of the crowd, they opened up the roof above him. After they had broken through, they let down the mat on which the paralytic was lying. When Jesus saw their faith, he said to the paralytic, "Child, your sins are forgiven."

MARK 2:1–5

Like the paralyzed man in this passage from the Gospel of Mark, we can look to Jesus for help in many situations of our life. Jesus knows that we all need to hear his message, "Your sins are forgiven."

Jesus said, "Your sins are forgiven."
Think of times you experienced forgiveness when you were growing up in your family—times when someone in your family had every reason to be angry with you, but instead hugged you and said, "It's going to be all right. I love you." Thank God for the times people you love showed you forgiveness when you were young.

Jesus said, "Your sins are forgiven."
Think of a time when you have experienced forgiveness from a friend. Think about a time when you told a friend, "I am so sorry." And your friend said, "I know. It's OK. It really is" in a way that let you keep on being friends. Thank God for the gift of your friend's forgiveness.

Jesus said, "Your sins are forgiven."
Think about your child who is preparing to celebrate the Sacrament of Penance and Reconciliation. Remember times when this child has forgiven you. Take some time to think of the ways this child shows his or her love for you. Thank God for the gift of your child's forgiveness and love.

Jesus said, "Your sins are forgiven."
Throughout your life, you've experienced forgiveness from different people, but who is it that you need to forgive? Who in your life has let you down? Who has taken you for granted? Who is it that you need to forgive before you become paralyzed from anger or hurt or lack of trust? What can you do to become reconciled? Ask God's help to make a first step.

Jesus said, "Your sins are forgiven."
Take a moment to think about yourself. Do you ever feel a need to forgive yourself? Think about the things that are hard for you to accept about yourself.

Now, imagine
looking into the eyes of Jesus and
hearing him say with gentle love,

"I love you my child,
your sins are forgiven."

People of healing and forgiveness

Think about special people in your life who have taught you about God's love and about true forgiveness and reconciliation. Write to your child telling about what you learned from them; then discuss your letter with your child.

Dear

Child's name

Something I have learned about God's love that I hope to pass on to you is

_____

_____

_____

_____

Something I have learned about forgiveness and reconciliation that I hope to pass on to you is

_____

_____

_____

_____

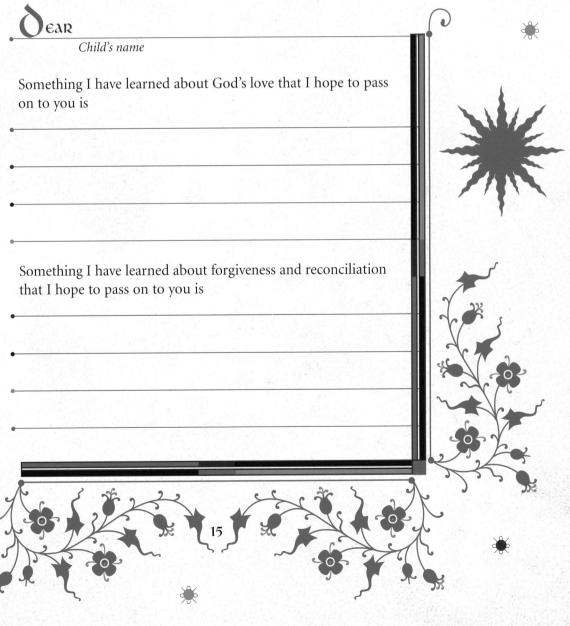

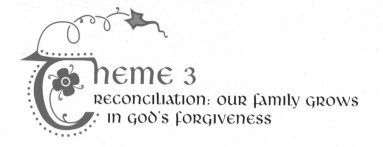

Theme 3
Reconciliation: our family grows in God's forgiveness

Our experiences of reconciliation invite us to reflect on areas of our life in need of God's healing and forgiveness. One way for your child to learn about the reality of sin and the consequences of making unloving choices is for you to share some of your own experiences.

Think about a time when you were young and you made an unloving choice, a time when you did something hurtful or wrong, a time when you needed and received forgiveness from someone else. What did you do? How did your actions affect others?

What did you do
to show you were sorry?

How did you know you were forgiven?

Share this story with your child.
Talk about the ways you showed you were sorry.

17

thinking back on the events of the day

From early in the Church's history, we have recognized the need to reflect on and pray about the events of the day so as to be more aware of God's presence and to name more clearly areas in need of God's healing grace. A daily time of self-reflection is an opportunity to recognize and remember God's loving care and God's hope that we will know and recognize the fullness of his love and forgiveness. It invites us into a reflection on the day's activities within a context of remembering God's love.

❋ **Stillness** We begin by taking a few moments to quiet ourselves and to remember that we are in God's presence. God's presence and steadfast love are always with us. We ask God to help us recognize and understand the presence of grace (God's life and love) in our lives. This is the gift of the Spirit, which is given to all who are baptized in Christ.

❋ **thankfulness** We remember those times of contentment or joy, opportunities for growth, or simply pleasure in the day. We give thanks to God for these gifts and the gift of life.

❋ **Reflection** Aware that God is constantly inviting us into relationship with himself and others, we think over the events and experiences of the day. We ask two questions:
  ◆ What in my day brought me closer to God and others?
  ◆ What in my day distanced me from God and others?
We then bring these times to God in prayer asking for the grace and help that we need.

❋ **hopefulness** We conclude by asking for God's blessings on the next day and for the grace to trust that the Spirit will guide and enlighten us.
  Based on MARGARET SILF *Inner Compass*
  (Chicago: Loyola Press, 1999.)

Reflecting on the day's experiences enhances our awareness of God's presence and opens our eyes to the areas in our lives that are in need of God's healing grace. Then we can be open to receive God's forgiveness and the grace to genuinely forgive others.

✳

Reflection on the first letter to the corinthians

Strive eagerly for the greatest spiritual gifts. But I shall show you a still more excellent way. If I speak in human and angelic tongues but do not have love, I am a resounding gong or a clashing cymbal. And if I have the gift of prophecy and comprehend all mysteries and all knowledge; if I have all faith so as to move mountains but do not have love, I am nothing. If I give away everything I own, and if I hand my body over so that I may boast but do not have love, I gain nothing.
    1 CORINTHIANS 12:31–13:3

Take time with your child to pray and reflect on this reading from First Corinthians. Use this reflection to help you talk honestly and gently with one another about things you do well and about ways you hope to change.

Love is patient,
Loving God, why do you have to ask me to be patient? Sometimes, I think it is hardest to be patient with the people in my own family. How do I act when someone I love is having a bad day? Do I understand when other people make a mistake?

Love is kind.
It seems so simple to be kind, God. Kindness is being thoughtful in little ways, like going out of your way to show someone you care about them. Do I do that? Do I pay attention to the needs of those around me?

[Love] is not jealous...
Jealous... Oh, that's not me, God! Is it? Do I ever worry that someone may have more than I have? Do I think more about what I can get from others, or more about what I can give? Help me God, to be generous, not jealous.

[Love] is not rude, it does not seek its own interests, it is not quick-tempered, it does not brood over injury,
Gracious God, you are asking me to be aware of and respond to the needs of others. Do I take time to think about how I can help others? And, what does this mean: "Love does not brood over injury"? Do I hold grudges, or can I forgive others when they let me down?

[Love] does not rejoice over wrongdoing but rejoices with the truth. It bears all things, believes all things, hopes all things, endures all things.... So faith, hope, love remain, these three; but the greatest of these is love.
   1 CORINTHIANS 13:4–7; 13

✳

LOVING GOD,
help us to make loving choices.

And when we do not,
bless us with the wisdom
to know what we must change and
with the courage to do it.

AMEN.

Becoming more loving

After reflecting together on the reading from First Corinthians, talk with your child about something you would like to change or work on in your life. For example, "I would really like to be more patient. I will do this by..."

PARENT: Something I would like to work on is

_____

PARENT: The ways I will try to do this are

_____

_____

Invite your child to do the same. Ask your child to name something he or she would like to work on or change. Suggest to your child that this may be something to talk to the priest about in the celebration of the Sacrament of Penance.

CHILD: Something I would like to work on is

_____

_____

CHILD: The ways I will try to do this are

_____

_____

_____

Participating in this sacrament for the first time is cause for celebrating and remembering. Take time with your child to talk about this experience.

ꬵill in the responses your child gives.

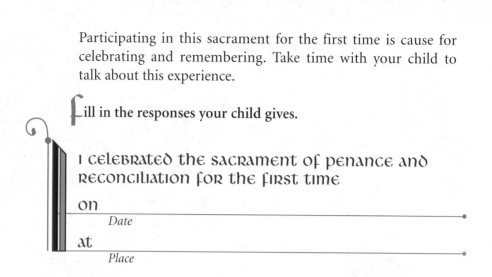

I celebrated the sacrament of penance and reconciliation for the first time

on _____
   Date

at _____
   Place

Describe the celebration.
The parts of the celebration that meant the most to me were

_____

_____

What I most want to remember about this day is

_____

_____

Use the next page for pictures or comments from family or friends.

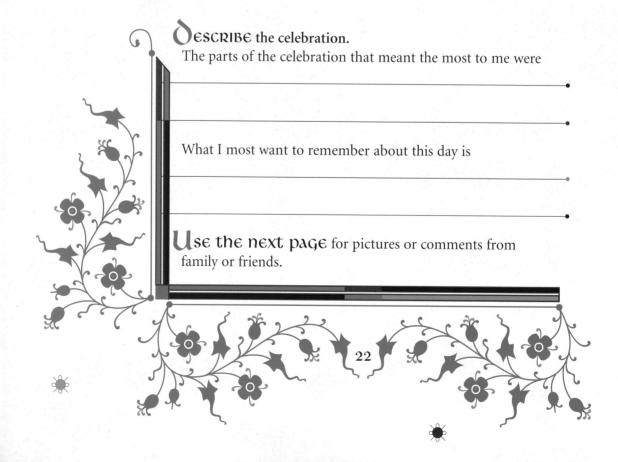

RECONCILIATION

Theme 4
eucharist: we enter the community through baptism

Record important memories of your child's baptism.

my child was baptized

on _____
   Date

at _____
   Name of Parish

in _____
   Name of city, state or province, country

What name did you give your child?

_____

Why did you choose this name?

_____

Who are your child's godparents?

_____

_____

Why did you choose them?

_____

_____

24

What special memories
do you have of your child's Baptism day?

Share these memories
of this Baptism day with your child.

Initiation into a community of faith

Anthropologists tell us that the initiation rites of a group, a tribe, or a people say a lot about the core characteristics of the group and the values it holds. Be it an isolated culture or an exclusive country club, the way people are received into a group forms and reflects the identity and values of the group.

The sacraments that celebrate our initiation as Christians—Baptism, Confirmation and Eucharist—call us to discipleship, community, and service.

* **Discipleship** Through Baptism, Christians enter into an extended discipleship to Jesus Christ. We enter into the lifelong process of learning not simply about Jesus Christ but how to live in a way that reflects the person and teaching of Jesus. To be a Christian is to be a disciple.

* **Community** This discipleship is supported and lived out within a parish—a community of faith. While we recognize that through Baptism we are baptized into Christ and into one people of God, we also see that this comes to expression within the local church. It is in our parish that we are nourished and strengthened and challenged to live out our discipleship every day.

* **Service** A fundamental expression of our discipleship in Jesus Christ is service to others. To live as Jesus did is to respond with love and concern to those around us. This is why the closing exchange of the Eucharist sends us forth to serve the Lord by serving those around us.

✳

Go in peace to love and serve the Lord.

Thanks be to God.

Reflection on the letter to the ephesians

I . . . urge you to live in a manner worthy of the call you have received, with all humility and gentleness, with patience, bearing with one another through love, striving to preserve the unity of the spirit through the bond of peace: one body and one Spirit, as you were also called to the one hope of your call; one Lord, one faith, one baptism; one God and Father of all, who is over all and through all and in all.
        Ephesians 4: 1–6

In this reading we are reminded of the importance of our Baptism and urged to live in a manner worthy of our call.

Baptism is a continuing call to live as Jesus lived and to love as Jesus loved. Think of someone who is living out his or her baptismal call in everyday life—a person whose faith and life you admire.

A person I know who acts as a follower of Christ in his/her everyday life is

In what ways does this person bring Jesus' love and presence to others?

In what ways is this person active in the Church?

_____

_____

_____

_____

_____

Something I have learned from this person is

_____

_____

_____

_____

_____

Others who have taught me about being a follower of Jesus are

_____

_____

_____

Our family's community of faith

When an infant is baptized, parents speak their beliefs and promises for their son or daughter. However, when children prepare to receive the Eucharist, they can speak about their beliefs and promises for themselves.

Talk with your child about Baptism and record his or her responses to the following:

Baptism is a call to love. Some of the people I love are

_____

Baptism is a call to be a follower of Jesus.
A way that I show that I am a follower of Jesus is

_____

Baptism is a call to belong to the Church.
A way that I show that I belong to the Church is

_____

A person who has helped me grow in my faith and learn about God is

_____

Something that this person has taught me is

_____

_____

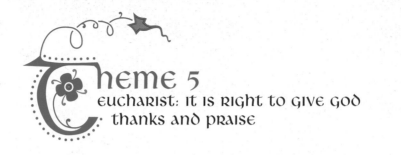

Theme 5
Eucharist: It is Right to Give God thanks and Praise

The word *Eucharist* means "giving thanks" and people who celebrate Eucharist are called to embrace an attitude of thankfulness, an "attitude of gratitude," in their everyday lives.

Reflect **on the following quotations:**

"Whatever we are waiting for—peace of mind, contentment, grace, the inner awareness of simple abundance—it will surely come to us, but only when we are ready to receive it with an open and grateful heart."

SARAH BAN BREATHNACH

What gifts has God blessed me with to help me be a good parent? What gifts am I grateful for?

What gifts do I ask God to bless me with—especially during this special time of sacramental formation for my child?

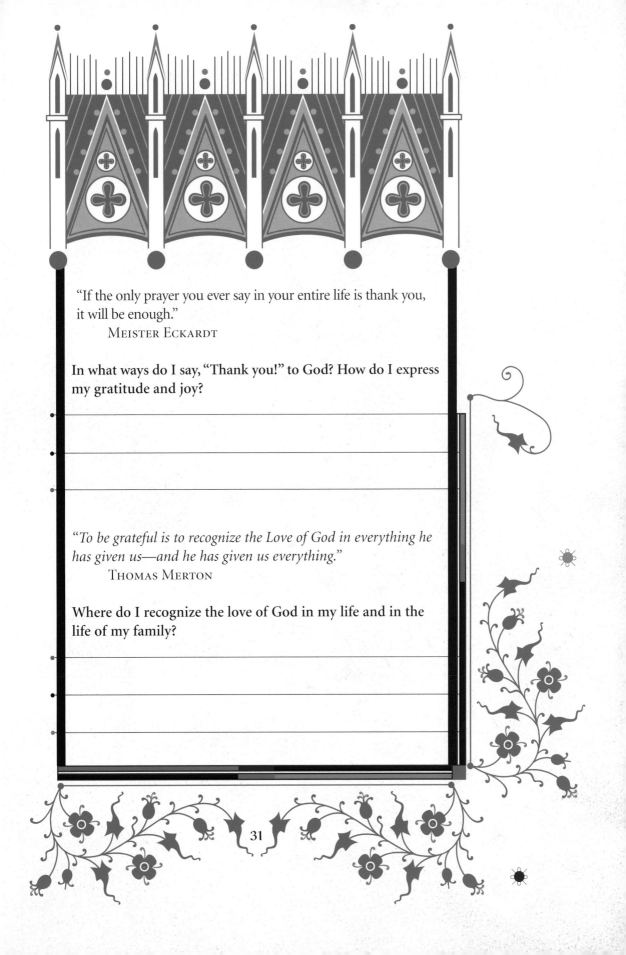

"If the only prayer you ever say in your entire life is thank you, it will be enough."

MEISTER ECKARDT

In what ways do I say, "Thank you!" to God? How do I express my gratitude and joy?

"To be grateful is to recognize the Love of God in everything he has given us—and he has given us everything."

THOMAS MERTON

Where do I recognize the love of God in my life and in the life of my family?

Saying "thank you" to God

This dialogue between presider and people begins the Eucharistic Prayer. It sets the tone for the entire prayer and reminds us that Eucharist means "to give thanks."

CELEBRANT: Lift up your hearts.
ALL: We lift them up to the Lord.
CELEBRANT: Let us give thanks to the Lord our God.
ALL: It is right to give him thanks and praise.

As a child heads out the door to a friend's house for dinner, a parent's reminder is often "Don't forget to say 'thank you!'" And while remembering to say "thank you" is important, we are trying to instill *both* good manners and the value of gratitude—gratitude not only for a good meal or a ride home, but for the gift of good friends, safe homes, and ultimately for life.

It is that larger sense of gratitude that is reflected in the above response "It is right to give him thanks and praise." In this statement, we affirm that all that we are and all we have are gifts from God. Our fundamental stance before God is one of gratitude.

At the heart of this stance of gratitude is the core Christian belief that God is always inviting each of us into an ever deeper relationship with him. The central dynamic of the relationship between God and each person is one of God's invitation and our response.

The "giving thanks" of Eucharist is our gratitude for the life, death and Resurrection of Jesus and for the presence of his Body and Blood. Eucharist is also about fostering an awareness of God's graciousness and responding with gratitude. As our Eucharistic prayer makes clear, even our desire to know God is itself God's gift.

We BRING to our weekly celebration of Eucharist the sense of gratitude for our families and for the gifts of the week. These are gathered in the opening of the Eucharistic Prayer when we respond that it is right to give God thanks and praise.

Reflection on the letter to the colossians

Let the word of Christ dwell in you richly, as in all wisdom you teach and admonish one another, singing psalms, hymns, and spiritual songs with gratitude in your hearts to God. And whatever you do, in word or in deed, do everything in the name of the Lord Jesus, giving thanks to God the Father through him.
  COLOSSIANS 3:16–17

In this reading we are reminded that we are to live with a sense of gratitude. We are called always to give thanks to God in the name of the Lord Jesus.

think about your child who will celebrate First Eucharist in the near future. What has this child taught you? What gifts has this child shared with you? What gifts will this child bring to the world?

WRITE A LETTER telling God why you are grateful for the gift of this child.

DEAR GOD,

I AM SO GRATEFUL FOR THE GIFT OF

Child's name

Praying together to our loving god

Asking God for help and giving thanks in gratitude come naturally when we realize our total dependence on him.

"Here are the two best prayers I know: "Help me, help me, help me," and "Thank you, thank you, thank you."
ANNE LAMOTT, *Traveling Mercies*

Follow this practice during bedtime prayer for a week with your child.

A Bedtime Prayer

"Help me, help me, help me."
God, three things I ask your help for today are
(Child responds first, then the parent.)

"Thank you, thank you, thank you."
God, three things I am thankful for today are
(Parent responds first, then the child.)

(Pray together)
Loving God, You know our needs better than we know our own. Help us to trust in your love and to open our hearts to your gifts. We pray this in the name of your Son, Jesus, who taught us how to live and love and pray.
Amen.

Over the course of the week, make a list of things for which you are grateful. When you get home from Mass on the weekend, review the list together.

Theme 6
Eucharist: Gathered to be sent

"Go in peace to love and serve the Lord."

Eucharist calls us to go out into the world to bring Jesus' love and presence to all in need.

It is in our families that we learn about caring for others, sharing what we have, trusting one another and responding to the needs of others. How has this been expressed in your family?

We share with others in need when we

_____

_____

We serve others in our parish and beyond when we

_____

_____

We show our respect for others when we

_____

_____

_____

We show our appreciation for people from different backgrounds and traditions when we

_____

_____

In what ways has your child

shown compassion and service to others?

Invitation to a meal

Throughout the Gospels, it seems that many significant events and important teachings are set within the context of a meal. And so it is appropriate that our own most significant encounter with Jesus takes place in a meal setting as well—in the Eucharist. A look at the role that meals played in Jesus' life helps us recognize the significance of the Eucharistic meal for us today.

* **Invitation** Stories of forgiveness and peace are expressed in stories of meals. Jesus' statement to the tax collector Zacchaeus, "Come down quickly for today I must stay at hour house," was heard by Zacchaeus as an invitation to conversion and to share what he had with the poor. Jesus makes clear that his invitation is open to everyone.

* **Response** In Luke's Gospel, Jesus tells us that many had been invited to a great feast only to send excuses for not coming on the day the feast was to begin. The host then invited the poor and lame—those who would never be invited to a feast—to come in and enjoy his food. Jesus makes clear in this story that God's invitation requires a response.

* **Recognition** At the end of Luke's Gospel we find the account of the dejected disciples on the road to Emmaus. They thought Jesus was dead. Although Jesus came to walk with them and tried to explain the meaning of his death and the promise of the Resurrection to them, they did not understand; they didn't even recognize him! But it was in the breaking of the bread that they were able to see him again. And in sharing that meal they were energized to go to the others and proclaim the new life that Jesus promised.

* **Jesus' gift of himself** And, most important, it was in the context of a meal that Jesus took bread and wine and, after giving thanks, said: *"This is my body which is for you.... This cup is the new*

covenant in my blood. Do this, as often as you drink it, in remembrance of me" (1 COR 11:24–25). Jesus is giving us his very self and will be with us always in this meal.

Reflecting on these stories helps us name some key themes that are to be present in our celebration of Eucharist: the invitation to share in the life of Jesus through the Eucharist is open to us. The invitation requires a response from us—not simply showing up but living lives that place our relationship with Jesus at the center. Through the Eucharistic meal, we are united in Jesus' death and Resurrection and sent to proclaim the reality of God's love for all people in word and action.

✳

Reflection on the gospel of john

Read the following gospel story, based on John 6: 1–14, with your child. Pause throughout to let your imaginations explore what the people in the story might have been thinking and feeling. Share your reflections with one another.

One day, Jesus went across the Sea of Galilee. He wanted to be alone, to take time to rest and pray. But a large crowd came searching for him. When the people found Jesus they pleaded, "Jesus, teach us more about the kingdom of heaven."

If you had been part of the crowd, what reasons would you have given for following Jesus?

By the time Jesus had finished teaching, it was late and everyone was very hungry. The disciples were worried.

39

"Jesus," Philip said, "These people have no food." "Feed them," Jesus said. "But Jesus, there's no food here," Philip cried. "Shouldn't we send them all away before darkness? No one could feed this crowd. There are just too many."

Philip seemed worried. If you were Philip, what would you have been thinking? How would you have responded?

One of the disciples, Andrew, said to Jesus, "There is a boy here who has a small basket of food. But what good is one basket of food for so many?" Jesus turned and asked the boy. "What do you have in your basket?" The boy gave his basket to Jesus. Inside were five loaves of bread and two small fish. "It's my supper, Jesus, but you may have it."

Imagine that you were the child. Do you think you would have offered to share your food?

Jesus thanked the boy and said, "Have the people prepare for a meal." The people sat down. There were about five thousand in number. Then Jesus took the loaves of bread, lifted them up to heaven and gave thanks. He blessed them and broke them into small pieces. "Here," he said. "Serve this food until everyone has eaten as much as they want." The disciples walked up and down the hillside, feeding everyone until they were full. The disciples ate too. When they had had their fill, Jesus said to his disciples, "Gather the fragments so that nothing will be wasted. Twelve baskets were filled to overflowing with the left over bread and fish. When the people saw this, they said, "Jesus is truly the One who is to come to save the world."

Jesus took the child's gift. He gave thanks. He blessed it and broke it. And thousands were fed. How do you think the boy felt when he saw this? What gifts do you have that you can share with others?

Sharing with others

After Jesus nourishes us in the Eucharist, we are asked to go out to be "bread for the world." Eucharist calls us to help feed those around us who are hungry. Some people are hungry for food, others are hungry for love, or care, or friendship.

Pray the following prayer together with your child.

PARENT: Some people in our world are hungry for food. They don't have enough to eat.
CHILD: Open our hands, God. Help us to share what we have with others.
PARENT: Some people in our world are hungry for care. They are sad or lonely. They need comfort and support.
CHILD: Open our eyes, God. Help us to see the needs of those around us.
PARENT: Some people in our world are hungry for friendship. They are excluded because others think they are "different" in some way.
CHILD: Open our hearts, God. Help us to share your love with others.

Together, make a commitment to bring the love of Jesus to someone in need.

Someone we know who is in need of help is

This person is hungry for (food, love, care, friendship, prayers)

We will help bring Jesus' love and care to this person by

41

Receiving Jesus in the Eucharist for the first time is cause for celebrating and remembering. Take time with your child to talk about this experience.

Fill in the responses your child gives.

I celebrated eucharist for the first time
on
_____
Date
at
_____
Place

Some of the people at the celebration were:

_____

_____

Describe the celebration.
The parts of the celebration that meant the most to me were:

_____

_____

What do you want to remember about this day?

_____

_____

Use the next page for pictures or comments from family or friends.

ðeo gratias

thanks be to god

A.D. MMIV